Elegy on the Death of César Chávez

by Rudolfo Anaya
illustrations by Gaspar Enriquez

Cinco Puntos Press
El Paso, Texas

Cinco Puntos Press would like to thank the Foundation for its support of this project, and we would especially like to thank Lorie De Leon of the Foundation for her help and support throughout this project.

First Edition
10   9   8   7   6   5   4   3   2   1

Library of Congress Cataloging-in-Publication Data

Anaya, Rudolfo A.
    Elegy on the death of César Chávez / by Rudolfo Anaya ; with illustrations by Gaspar Enriquez.
        p.   cm.
        Summary: A poem eulogizing the Mexican American labor activist César Chávez and his work helping organize migrant farm workers.
        ISBN 0-938317-80-6 (paperback)
        1. Chávez, César, 1927--Juvenile poetry. 2. Mexican American migrant agricultural laborers--Juvenile poetry. 3. Migrant agricultural laborers--Juvenile poetry. 4. Mexican Americans--Juvenile poetry. 5. Labor leaders--Juvenile poetry. 6. Children's poetry, American. [1. Chávez, César, 1927--1993 Poetry. 2. Labor leaders--Poetry. 3. Mexican Americans--Poetry. 4. Migrant labor--Poetry. 5. American poetry.] I. Enriquez, Gaspar, 1942- ill. II. Title.

    PS3551.N27 E44 2000
    811'.54--dc21
                                                                                        00-024832

Many thanks to photographers Alan Pogue and José Galvez for images used in building the collage illustrations by Gaspar Enriquez. In addition, we would like to thank Thomas Featherstone from the Walter Reuther Library at Wayne State University for his assistance in providing images from the United Farm Worker archives that are housed in that library. • ¡Hats off to Ann Marie Enriquez! • A warm welcome to the publishing business for Ruby Alarcon, on this her first book. Thanks Ruby Ruby. • Printed in Hong Kong. Thanks, Suzy.

Book and cover design by Geronimooo Design Inc. of El Paso, Texas.
Thanks to you, Geronimo, for your continuing support of and friendship towards Cinco Puntos Press.

This book is funded in part by generous support from the National Endowment for the Arts.

NATIONAL
ENDOWMENT
FOR ❦ THE
ARTS

Elegy on the Death of César Chávez

I weep for Adonais

—he is dead!

O, weep for Adonais!

though our tears

Thaw not the frost which

binds so dear a head!

—Percy Bysshe Shelley

From Adonias, An Elegy on the Death of John Keats

This earth he loved so well is dry and mourning

César is dead,
> And we have wept for him until our eyes are dry,
> Dry as the fields of California that
>> He loved so well and now lie fallow.
> Dry as the orchards of Yakima, where dark buds
>> Hang on trees and do not blossom.
> Dry as el Valle de Tejas where people cross
>> Their foreheads and pray for rain.

This earth he loved so well is dry and mourning
> For César has fallen, our morning star has fallen.

...this man who was a guide across fields of toil

The messenger came with the sad news of his death—
O, kill the messenger and steal back the life
Of this man who was a guide across fields of toil.
Kill the day and stop all time, stop la muerte
Who has robbed us of our morning star, that
Luminous light that greeted workers as they
Gathered around the dawn campfires.

How can this man who moved like the light of justice die?

Let the morning light of Quetzacóatl and Christian saint
　　Shine again. Let the wings of the Holy Ghost unfold
　　And give back the spirit it took from us in sleep.

Across the land we heard las campanas doblando:
　　Ha muerto César, Ha muerto César.

How can the morning star die? we ask. How can
　　This man who moved like the light of justice die?

Hijo de la Virgen de Guadalupe, hombre de la gente,
　　You starved your body so we might know your spirit.

VIVA CESAR CHAVEZ
1927-1993

César had awakened to a greater dream

The days do carry hope, and the days do carry treason.
O, fateful day, April 23, 1993, when our morning
Star did not rise and we knew that in his sleep
César had awakened to a greater dream.

And we, left lost on this dark, dry Earth,
Cursed the day la muerte came to claim
The light within his noble body.

A scourge on the oppressors of the poor

He was a wind of change that swept over our land.
From the San Joaquín Valley north to Sacramento
From northwest Yakima to el Valle de Tejas
From el Valle de San Luis to Midwest fields of corn
He loved the land, he loved la gente.

His name was a soft breeze to cool the campesino's sweat
A scourge on the oppressors of the poor.

...children uneducated in a land grown fat with greed

Now he lies dead, and storms still rage around us.
The dispossessed walk hopeless streets,
Campesinos gather by roadside ditches to sleep,
Shrouded by pesticides, unsure of tomorrow,
Hounded by propositions that keep their children
Uneducated in a land grown fat with greed.

Yes, the arrogant hounds of hate
Are loose upon this land again, and César
Weeps in the embrace of La Virgen de Guadalupe,
Still praying for his people.

"Rise, mi gente, rise," he prays.

...like the righteous thunder of summer storms

His words echo across the land, like the righteous Thunder of summer storms, like the call of a Warrior preparing for the struggle. I hear his Voice in fields and orchards, in community halls, In schools, churches, campesino homes and Presidential palaces.

"Rise, mi gente, rise!"

Rise together and build a new society

That was his common chant. Rise and organize,

Build the House of the Workers.

Build the House of Justice now!

Do not despair in violence and abuse.

Rise together and build a new society.

Build a new democracy, build equality,

And build a dream for all to share.

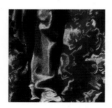

I hear the sound of marching feet

His voice stirs me now, and I rise from my grief.
I hear the words of the poet cry:
"Peace, peace! He is not dead, he doth not sleep—
He hath awakened from the dream of life."

I hear César calling for us to gather.
I hear the call to a new Huelga,
I hear the sound of marching feet
The guitarra strums of the New Movimiento
The old and young, rich and poor, all move
To build the House of Justice of César's dream!

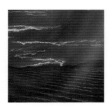

He lives in the hearts of those who loved him

The trumpet of righteousness calls us to battle!
And the future opens itself like the blossom
That is his soul, the fruit of his labor.
He calls for us to share in the fruit.

"He lives, he wakes—'tis Death is dead, not he;
Mourn not for Adonais."

Do not weep for César, for he is not dead.
He lives in the hearts of those who loved him,
Worked and marched and ate with him, and those
Who believed in him.

Rise not against each other, but for each other

His disciples know he is not dead,
    For in the dawn we see the morning star!
    El lucero de Dios!
    Light comes to illuminate the struggle,
    And bless the work yet to be done.

Throughout Aztlán we call the young to gather:
    Rise and put aside violence and temptations.
    Rise and be swept up by the truth of his deeds,
    Rise not against each other, but for each other,
    Rise against the oppressors who take your sweat
    And labor and sell it cheap.

    "Rise, mi gente, rise!"

Listen to his voice in the wind

Our César has not died!

He is the light of the new day.

He is the rain that renews parched fields.

He is the hope that builds the House of Justice.

He is with us! Here! Today!

Listen to his voice in the wind.

He is the spirit of Hope,

A movement building to sweep away oppression!

His spirit guides us in the struggle.

Let us join his spirit to ours!

Sing with me. Sing all over this land!

"Rise, mi gente, rise!

Rise, me gente, rise!"

A Note from Rudolfo Anaya

When César Chávez died, a shroud of mourning fell over all who knew, loved, and respected him. We knew we had lost a special man from our community, one who had influenced so many lives. We didn't have to know him personally to feel the loss, we knew that his life had bettered the lives of many farm workers.

Who was this man whose death filled us with grief? César Chávez, named after his grandfather, was born March 31, 1927, on a farm near Yuma, Arizona. His grandparents had migrated from Mexico and settled near Yuma where they built a farm house and worked the land. During the Great Depression of the 1930s, the farm was lost to unpaid taxes, and César's family became migrant workers in the vineyards of California.

Living conditions for migrant workers were horrible. The poorly paid farm workers lived in shacks and under bridges. César's family moved so much he attended dozens of different schools and finally dropped out in the eighth grade. Migrant workers faced discrimination at every turn.

By the time he was 15, César was picking crops with Filipinos, Mexicans, African-Americans and Anglos. At night he slept in filthy, over-crowded labor camps. He was working in the vineyards of the San Joaquín valley when the workers were sprayed with toxic pesticides by a crop duster. César saw tragedy strike the workers time and again.

After serving in World War II, César returned to marry his sweetheart, Helen Fabela. They lived in the barrio Sal Si Puedes. César began to read the writings of people who said every worker has the right to decent wages and living conditions. He read about Mahatma Gandhi's non-violent marches and strikes, and he knew of Martin Luther King's civil rights struggle for equality.

The hunger and suffering of the farm workers motivated César to leave his work in the fields and start registering people to vote. The more farm workers he met, the more he realized the real need was for a farm workers' union. César, along with Dolores Huerta, decided to organize the farm workers. On September 30, 1962, the National Farm Workers Association was founded in Fresno with chapters of farm workers throughout the vast San Joaquín Valley.

In the fall of 1965, Filipino farm workers went out on strike. On September 16, César held a meeting of his union and a vote was taken to strike in support of the Filipinos. The cry *¡Huelga!-Strike!* filled Our Lady of Guadalupe church. On April 24, 1966, the union ended a 340-mile march from Delano to Sacramento. The nation now knew the name of César Chávez.

During the '70s, I was fortunate to have attended conferences where César spoke. Sitting in the audience, I saw him from afar. Even from a distance his charisma was evident; he could galvanize any audience. I, like millions of others, knew his work. Perhaps that is what defines any person, their work. The legacy of César Chávez is the tireless effort he exerted so that those who toil in the fields might live better lives.

This man who gave so much for others should not be forgotten. To honor César, we don't have to make him a saint. We have to honor the good he accomplished. César Chávez didn't work to make himself great, he didn't work to acquire fame or worldly possessions, he worked for la gente.

There are many ways to honor the spirit of the man. I did it by writing this elegy. We can honor him by dedicating some part of our lives to helping others. Getting an education and serving our families and communities also honors César.

So does knowing our history and the accomplishments of our great men and women.

The elegy is a way of expressing one's grief and telling something of a person's life. When I heard the news of César's death, I was saddened. I could feel the grief his family and close friends were experiencing. He was so active in his work, he still had so many plans, so many projects that needed to be finished. I felt I had lost a good friend.

I'm sure my feelings were shared by millions in this country and all over the world who knew of his work. He was the most respected leader of our generation. We not only respected him, we loved him. He was the prized symbol of our community.

But he was more than a symbol and a hero. He was a family man, a husband, a father. He came from a humble, hard-working family. He knew the hard work of the fields. He lived and worked with the campesinos. It was that experience in life that molded his spirit and allowed him to become a leader for the people. He was a man who understood that by organizing the workers, their lives could be bettered.

When I heard of his death, I felt I needed to say something about his life. I needed to give expression to my feelings. So the elegy poured out, my gift for César. Writing the elegy not only honors César, it was a way for me to deal with his death.

This poem is only one small offering. People have honored César in many other ways. Perhaps the greatest honor is that his work continues. The people at the United Farm Workers of America (UFW) continue in their efforts to help the farm workers. A line in the poem states that we must rise from our grief to continue the work.

More and more our society is divided between those who are rich and those who are poor. Poverty, lack of housing, low wages, inhumane working conditions, and lack of educational opportunities are barriers that destroy the spirit. César understood this—that's why he organized people. We, too, must fight against injustices that rob the spirit.

There is a lot of work to be done if we are to continue César's battle against injustice. We must all come together—from all cultural backgrounds—to fight for equality. And the war is not yet won. Too many people still suffer from unequal opportunities. Too many spirits are still crushed by poverty.

While writing this poem, I came to the realization that although César is gone, his spirit lives on. His spirit is there to nourish us. César is still leading the battle for human rights. This is a battle we can all join.

Build the house of justice, the poem says in the end. Each one of us has a role in building that house. Each one of us must make a commitment to build a better society. Yes, we must organize. We must work together. We must fight against oppression. In this way we honor César and all the good men and women who have struggled to better our lives.

—Rudolfo Anaya

A Chronology of the Life of César Chávez

1927, March 31

Césario Estrada Chávez is born near Yuma, Arizona.

1937

After César's father, Librado, is forced from his farm, César and his family become migrant workers in California.

1942

César quits school after the eighth grade and works in the fields full-time to help support his family.

1944

César joins the U.S. Navy during World War II and serves in the western Pacific. Just before shipping out, César is arrested in a segregated Delano, California movie theater for sitting in the "Whites Only" section.

1948

César marries Helen Fabela. They eventually have eight children.

Late 1940s

César begins studying the social teachings of the Catholic Church.

1952

Community organizer Fred Ross discovers the young farm worker laboring in apricot orchards outside San Jose, California, and recruits him into the Community Service Organization (CSO).

1952–1962

Together with Fred Ross, César organizes 22 CSO chapters across California in the 1950s. Under César's leadership, the CSO helps Latinos become citizens, registers them to vote, battles police brutality and presses for paved streets and other barrio improvements.

1962, March 31

César resigns as president from the CSO after its rejection of his proposal to organize farm workers. César and Dolores Huerta, along with the support of his wife Helen, decide to resign from the CSO to establish the National Farm Workers Association (NFWA). César and his family move to Delano and César dedicates himself full-time to organizing farm workers.

1962, September 30

The first convention of the National Farm Workers Association is convened in Fresno, California.

1962–1965

Often baby-sitting his youngest children as he drives to dozens of farm worker towns, César painstakingly builds up the membership of his infant union.

1965, September 16

On Mexican Independence Day, the NFWA, with 1,200-member families, votes to join a strike against Delano-area grape growers already begun that month by the mostly Filipino American members of the Agricultural Workers Organizing Committee, AFL-CIO (AWOC). Thus begins the five-year Delano Grape Strike.

1966, March–April

César and a band of strikers embark upon a 340-mile Peregrinación (or Pilgrimage) from Delano to the steps of the state Capitol in Sacramento to draw national attention to the suffering of farm workers. During the pilgrimage and after a four-month boycott, Dolores Huerta, vice-president of the NFWA, negotiates the first genuine contract in the history of the U.S. between a grower, Schenley Vineyards, and farm workers.

1966, Spring–Summer

A boycott of DiGiorgio Fruit Corporation forces the giant grape grower to agree to an election among its workers. The company brings in the Teamsters Union to oppose the NFWA. The NFWA and the Filipino American AWOC merge to form the United Farm Workers and the union affiliates with the AFL-CIO, the national labor federation. DiGiorgio workers vote for the UFW.

1967

The UFW strikes the Giumarra Vineyards Corporation, California's largest table-grape grower. In response to a UFW boycott, other grape growers allow Giumarra to use their labels. The UFW begins a boycott of all California table grapes.

1967–1970

Hundreds of grape strikers fan out across North America to organize an international grape boycott. Millions of Americans rally to La Causa, the farm workers' cause.

1968, February–March

César fasts for 25 days to rededicate his movement to nonviolence. U.S. Senator Robert F. Kennedy joins 8,000 farm workers and supporters at a mass where César breaks his fast, calling the weakened farm labor leader "one of the heroic figures of our time."

1970, Spring–Summer

As the boycott continues picking up steam, most California table-grape growers sign UFW contracts.

1970, Summer

To keep the UFW out of California lettuce and vegetable fields, most Salinas Valley growers sign contracts with the Teamsters Union. Some 10,000 Central Coast farm workers respond by walking out on strike. César calls for a nationwide boycott of lettuce.

1970, December 10–24

César is jailed in Salinas, California for refusing to obey a court order to stop the boycott against Bud Antle lettuce. Coretta Scott King and Ethel Kennedy visit César in jail.

Chronology © United Farm Workers (www.ufw.org), César Chávez Foundation, P.O. Box 62, Keene, CA 93531.

1971

The UFW moves from Delano to its new headquarters at La Paz in Keene, California, southeast of Bakersfield. With table and wine-grape contracts and some agreements covering vegetable workers, UFW membership grows to around 80,000.

1972

The UFW is chartered as an independent affiliate by the American Federation of Labor-Congress of Industrial Organizations (AFL-CIO); it becomes the United Farm Workers of America, AFL-CIO.

1972, May 11–June 4

César fasts for 25 days in Phoenix over a just-passed Arizona law banning the right of farm workers to strike or boycott.

1973, Spring–Summer

When the UFW's three-year table-grape contracts come up for renewal, growers instead sign contracts with the Teamsters without an election or any representation procedure. A bitter three-month strike by grape workers begins in California's Coachella and San Joaquín valleys. Thousands of strikers are arrested for violating anti-picketing injunctions, hundreds are beaten, dozens are shot and two are murdered. In response to the violence, César calls off the strike and begins a second grape boycott.

1975, June

After Jerry Brown becomes governor, the boycott convinces growers to agree to a state law guaranteeing California farm workers the right to organize and bargain with their employers. César gets the landmark Agricultural Labor Relations Act through the state legislature.

1975–1976, September–January

Hundreds of elections are held. The UFW wins the majority of the elections in which it participates. The Agricultural Labor Relations Board (ALRB) which enforces the law briefly shuts down after running out of money, and pro-grower lawmakers refuse to approve an emergency appropriation.

Mid-to-late 1970s

The UFW continues winning elections and signing contracts with growers. In 1977, the Teamsters Union signs a "jurisdictional" agreement with the UFW and agrees to leave the fields. In 1978, the UFW calls off its boycotts of grapes, lettuce and Gallo wine.

1979, January–October

In a bid to win decent wages and benefits, the UFW strikes several major lettuce and vegetable growers up and down the state. Rufino Contreras, a 27-year-old striker, is shot to death in an Imperial Valley lettuce field by grower foremen.

1979, September

After a strike and boycott, the UFW wins its demands for a significant pay raise and other contract improvements from Sun Harvest, the nation's largest lettuce producer. Other growers also soon settle.

Early 1980s

With election victories and contract negotiations, the number of farm workers protected by UFW contracts grows to about 45,000.

1982

Republican George Deukmejian is elected California governor with one million dollars in grower campaign contributions.

1983–1990

Deukmejian begins shutting down enforcement of the state's historic farm labor law. Thousands of farm workers lose their UFW contracts. Many are fired and blacklisted. Fresno-area dairy worker Rene Lopez, 19, is shot to death by grower agents after voting in a 1983 union election. César declares a third grape boycott in 1984.

1986

César kicks off the "Wrath of Grapes" campaign to draw public attention to the pesticide poisoning of grape workers and their children.

1988, July–August

At age 61, Chávez conducts his last—and longest—public fast for 36 days in Delano to call attention to farm workers and their children stricken by pesticides.

1992, Spring–Summer

Working with UFW First Vice President Arturo Rodriguez, César leads vineyard walkouts in the Coachella and San Joaquín valleys. As a result, grape workers win their first industry-wide pay hike in eight years.

1993, April 23

César Chávez dies peacefully in his sleep in San Luis, Arizona.

1993, April 29

40,000 mourners march behind César's casket during funeral services in Delano.

1994, March–April

On the first anniversary of César's passing, 17,000 farm workers and supporters march to the steps of the state Capitol in Sacramento, completeing a 340-mile pilgrimage and repeating the 1966 march.

1994, August 8

President Bill Clinton posthumously presents the Medal of Freedom—America's highest civilian honor—to César Chávez. His widow, Helen, receives the medal during a White House ceremony.

One way of continuing the work of César Chávez is to support the good work of the United Farm Workers Union and the César E. Chávez Foundation. To get more information, check out the UFW website at www.ufw.org or the Foundation at www. cesarechavezfoundation.org. Another way is to become involved in the struggles of conscience in your neighborhood and city.

The paintings by Gaspar Enriquez illustrating Rudolfo Anaya's poem are in the permanent collection of the El Paso Museum of Art and are available as a traveling exhibition. For more information, contact the museum's curator at 915-532-1707.

Multicultural and Bilingual Books for Children of All Ages
From Cinco Puntos Press

Selavi, That Is Life: A Haitian Story of Hope
Written and illustrated by Youme Landowne

¡Sí, Se Puede! / Yes, We Can!
By Diana Cohn and illustrated by Francisco Delgado

A Gift from Papá Diego / Un regalo de Papá Diego
By Benjamin Alire Sáenz and illustrated by Geronimo Garcia

The Treasure on Gold Street / el Tesoro en la Calle Oro
By Lee Merrill Byrd and illustrated by Antonio Castro L.

The Day It Snowed Tortillas / El día que nevaron tortillas: Folktales in Spanish and English
By Joe Hayes with illustrations by Antonio Castro L.

El Cucuy: A Bogeyman Cuento in English and Spanish
By Joe Hayes and illustrated by Honorio Robledo

Cinco Puntos Press
701 Texas Avenue
El Paso, TX 79901
800-566-9072
www.cincopuntos.com